Blue Halo

Also by Toni Thomas:

Chosen
    Brick Road Poetry Press

Fast as Lightening
    Gribble Press

Walking on Water
    Finishing Line Press

Ace Raider of the Unfathomable Universe
    Annalese Press

Blue Halo

Toni Thomas

First published in 2016 by Annalese Press
134 Towngate
Netherthong
Holmfirth
West Yorkshire HD9 3XZ

Copyright © 2016 Toni Thomas

Please Note
All characters and situations appearing
in these pages are in the service of poetry.
Any resemblance to real persons,
living or dead, is purely coincidental.

All rights reserved. No part of this publication may be reproduced, stored, or transmitted in any form, or by any means electronic, mechanical or photocopying, recording or otherwise, without the express written permission of the publisher.

Cover photograph and artwork by Peter Wadsworth

British Library Cataloguing-in-Publication Data
A catalogue record for this book is available on request from the British Library.

ISBN 978-0-9956652-1-7

for Steve

Acknowledgements

My deep gratitude goes to not only the amazing world class poets I have been very fortunate to work with, but also to the personal friends who have shown me endless support and encouragement and ultimately made this work possible. Among them a special thanks to Jan, Sophie, Bob M., Peter R., Michael, my children Ahven and Fergus, my dad, and my mother who is long gone but always with me. Thanks to Keith at Brick Road Poetry Press, Gribble Press, and Finishing Line Press for taking a chance on me. A special thanks to Peter Wadsworth at Annalese Press for his endless belief in the quality of these poems and willingness to publish this collection along with a companion book of poems entitled *Ace Raider of the Unfathomable Universe*.

And finally my appreciation goes to my brother who I miss deeply and who touched my life in indelible ways.

"Brother, today I sit on the brick bench of the house,
Where you make a bottomless emptiness.
I remember we used to play at this hour,
and mama caressed us ...

.....Listen brother, don't be late coming out.
All right? Mama might worry."

Cesar Vallejo
from "To My Brother Miquel in Memoriam"

Contents

Part One *Missing*

All my life	1
We are on a carousel	2
In the bottomless of your heart	3
In the watch keeper's anthology	4
You wear a limp corsage	5
You tell me money talks	6
In the causeway	7
We were thirsting for something	8
In the land of fugitives	9
My only brother has gone missing	10

Part Two *Orphaned Waifs*

You have to know the boy	11
Some things break too soon	12
We are playing a word game	13
You don't startle the dark into pissing	15
You rock peddle your words	17
You wear cologne	20
Your all wheel drive	22
It's hard to be sleepless	24
You have found a circuitous way to paradise	25
The night you try to commit suicide	27

Part Three *Patronage*

Sometimes we write others off	29
You will barely eat the Christmas meal	31
You hold an invisible guardrail	33
Sometimes you and I don't seem alike	34
The day journey is hard	36
Your body is tired	38
You garble your words	39
They want your name	40

Part Four *Pallbearer*

The crops went fallow	43
You will never grow old	44
They are trying to keep your flesh pink	46
You want me to be a pallbearer	47
I comb the field	48
I do not want to suds the past	49
Your body will be burned	50
You were buried	53
The breakfast of the dead	54

Part Five *A Praxis of Want*

We have bought cast hearts	55
Your voice	57
February marches into April	59
It won't do any good	60

I'm kissing your hallelujah chorus	61
You are *not* knee deep in hand grenades	63
It is your birthday	64
Your ashes are sealed	66
This day holds the memory	67
If the sun blessed your face	69
Some of us walk the world	71
The auburn in your hair	74

Part Six   *The Diurnal Sunset*

The diurnal sunset	77
Some people burn so bright	78
Your hair is windswept	79
You are a pebble field	80
Your death is a broad machine	81
Do you still peel the top off	82
Some days you aerate the yard	84
When I braille you in the dark	85
The ghosts of the dark	87
The dark can be blinding	88
It is hard to make a life fit	89
Who calls the dark out of hiding	91
It's time for you to start	92

When you told me you wanted

to go back to her
our mother who died too young
said *she is waiting for me, don't try to interfere
know this is what I want
I'm tired sister*

in my heart of hearts I knew already
I had lost you
that you were on your way home

but I couldn't let you go yet
talked with you on the phone for over an hour
in an anonymous car park
cried, implored
till finally you gave us your motel address
on the pretext of a final farewell

and on that day, at that hour
a hand longer than my own
seemed to save you

and I told you - whatever happens
someday I am going to write a book of your life
and you said *if you ever do, tell it straight*

and so brother, who has taken the flowers
from the right ventricle of my heart
as promised
this book is for you
and I will tell about it.

Part One

Missing

All my life

I've wanted to be the girl
with the wick
who blue halos pain

pins your honey heart to my sleeve
as if you never pilfer
drop dead in the dark.

Sometimes life is squeamish
detonates the trees
absolves fate with linguistics.

I tattoo the yard in bachelor buttons
scratch your name in the dirt
curl my past into an antidote

squeeze out your pyrotechnics

lure your preposterous
into emerald.

We are on a carousel

you carouse with the ponies
look for the fastest ride
a Flemish bride
smooth mane.

Crowded as a racecourse
the country of flowers
escapes me.

I watch you yank
tug on your horse's mouthpiece
leave me behind

as if strident hands
embalm the dark
pebble a past

deliver hasty love notes

a kiss so delinquent
it fortune tells no rain.

In the bottomless of your heart

there are pull toys and inertia
a briny past
crooked road to the beach

there are hereafters
and peony
an hourglass of field daisy

he loves me, loves me not
and *Look – I can see all the way to the coast!*

and *give me a break*

and *your eyes*
    your eyes

they are bluer than the Danube!

In the bottomless of your heart
you meet god daily
on the elevator
woe her

recite the *Our Father*
to the fisted arms of the night
memorize the storybook of love
in her green kerchief.

In the watch keeper's anthology

we are all on a timetable toward death
trees weep
cows are exiled
the car with the pearly wheels is etched
into the assassin's notebook
you mix white powder
into Molotov cocktails
learn a new language for love
annihilation

want to see past the woman with two kids
who deals a good business, never gets caught
want to see past broken jobs, whittled health care
the state penitentiary
see past the mall's city size parking lot
but your heart refuses to carry you.

In the watch keeper's notebook
we are a funeral march wedded to bright wheels
dangle our blue charms, incense
fancy phone
forget something at the end
more eventful
claims.

You wear a limp corsage

the sickly yellow of gutted snow
a poor man's urinal

close my eyes and I can hear
your body call
wander the stairs
the blind leading the blind
through white powdered rooms
puddled cream.

Please tell me my mother's favorite
is not the big boy grown sickly
his pickled heart
run amuck in our street malls

how many times have I said –
don't leave me
don't leave me

as you disappear
through the revolving door
my one and only
one and only.

You tell me money talks

can twirl on a rope
taunt antelope
staple a purse
everywhere catalogs of shoes
beach condos at the coast.

See how the gradients of the dark
perform when we flash
recite the names of presidents
shrink wrap hope
go house to house with their collection box
marry the blue salver
make a killing on real estate

how you stay unplused
glad to see the yard's not waxed
coin feed your gorilla.

In the causeway

between loss and hope
that gutter region
the rain seeps

carries our toy boats
hyacinth
catalogs of the maimed

carries our tinsel
Caruso shoes.

In the causeway
a boy waits.
He is shirtless
in need of a sea.
I want to talc his body
but my hands go missing.

Is this the way the dead
minister to the dark

is this what loss breeds?

We were thirsting for something

You were thirsting for light
dice rolls, a lap dog
Crème Brulee on a shoestring
the way crack feels when it fries your brain
erases the equation tables
as if nothing has abandoned us
and the next and the next
will see us home
keep the dark from creeping.

See how the sun feels hard as a nutshell
gym workout
is all volition
how the past putrefies
and my father's voice bellows
its angular mineshaft

see the way you flee from me
month after month
year after year
while God sits
glued to the underside
of your tray table

how this white powdered lullaby
road to oblivion
dislodges our dead mother
crucifies.

In the land of fugitives

we emerald city the dark
till it doesn't speak dirty.

The city of light grows
sepia toned
no longer in need
of a face wash.

How many times have I come to you
lace and attrition
dry moped disaster
wanted to hear in your hands
the birds sing?

My only brother has gone missing

snatched away
his sullen
and artifice

his hurting
small boy
generous heart

the way
the whistle blower toots
more and more
more and more

till nothing
is left.

Part Two

Orphaned Waifs

You have to know the boy

who lit our porch roof big as a Christmas pageant
made a Halloween fantasy trail with
an axe murderer in blue jeans
could diagnose a car problem in two minutes
eat fire
fan lightning bugs till they came straight
into his glass jar.

You have to know the boy who didn't understand life
didn't believe it was just what we're told
the straight lines and no questions
the way we pulverize what is not neat
that angular piece of the pie
up against our unwilling.

You have to understand a father's warfare
kerosened yard beetles
words that ricochet off walls

how fire can warm or eat us
take our clothes, our life, our loves
raise a house, a field

till they're ash.

Some things break too soon

sit on the verge of disaster
are a pirate's penance
sulky clown, doll with the overcast eye
toys that need more love
hold delicate limbs
Buzz Light-year pajamas
blue paralysis
an impatient view of identical condos.

Some toys are pantomimes and fair-thee-wells
boot spurs, a stage set where dynamite
explodes in a war zone
are love triangles
spirals of the girl with the loose curls
dancing a polka

they are card tricks, painted eggs
metal trucks with a flamethrower

are blue gyros, a frog prince
sick pups we nurse with a milk bottle
the beheaded king
plastic pistol

lassos that can grab somebody's neck
somebody's neck
when the room wears grey Christmas
when everything's nested in ice

and strangle.

We are playing a word game

you spell *amaryllis*
chide that we are neck and neck
for the big prize – free pizza,
I try *Cassiopeia*, then *conundrum*.
You are my only brother and I have
always been a smuck when it comes
to attempts at beating you

whether its words, poker, spades
ping pong balls looped over the net
tennis matches alongside my father.
Not that slaughter seems to trouble
afterall, you are my father's child
and being a tyrant means no remorse

there are slams I can't beat
balls so deadly, they pulverize the net
the speed of light flattens.

We are playing a word game.
You reach for another Pepsi
tell me I'll be paying for the pizza

that sometimes when the cough is bad
you feel like a three fisted kid
the dark gets scary
and you see our mom coming
as if god occupies her hill
tell me she's not past beautiful

cotton petal pushers, page boy, barefoot
not to worry for you.

And then I am sad. Don't want to play anymore.
Say– *Chris– you can't leave me. Can't can't can't.*
but less than six months from now
you will.

You don't startle the dark into pissing

moccasin your feet, walk quiet through corridors
keep the kitchen machinery from hissy
play more than blue notes on your Gibson
lathe soft words on the sad dog
bury his want with more than a dry bone

tickle, ruffle his belly
remind him of white sand beaches
squirrels that need him
yard birds
the dog down the block
who's up all hours in a panic
howling for love.

You always were the storyteller
more than the guy down on his luck
stuck with the $32,000 back surgery
who pawns Seiko watches
is the reliable worker
April Fool's prankster
doesn't always *buckle up for safety*
turn the other cheek
while the city burns.

You are my mother's son risen early
who slips out the screen door
watches the sun climb
likes colored pinwheels, cotton candy, rollercoasters
doesn't complain about cheap food
the used car
befriends the child that nobody else sees

will go a long way to say your peace
to the boss, co-workers
be frank about work ethics, decency
not just wonder about where
the American Dream has fled.

You rock peddle your words

call me over
to calm the lonely
take you to the emergency room
if the chest pain gets worse.

I have been here before
don't want to go
if that shit is happening
am scared of your state
have you promise on the phone
you will be done using.
I am the girl who lives in a vacuum
is petrified to watch scary films
see you slur into oblivion.

Sometimes we lie to get company
or else fudge the facts.
When I arrive you are still using the pipe
high as a kite
say you can't waste what's left
spill out your life story in halting words
that ask careful listening

and I feel like I am in a horror story
with blue machetes, truculent drug dealers
ransoms and stolen cars
threats to break your arms
hammer the window
if the rest of the money doesn't arrive.

And we talk about the past
the way you are killing yourself
and how I can't bear to watch
and we talk about my father's short fuse
his years in an orphanage
your memories of our mother
how she loved with no strings
and you'll be going back
and we talk about your sex life
which I don't want to hear
what crack does to it
and in your sad beautiful blue eyes
I witness your lonely
your broken dreams and busted heart
and you want to know about my dating
and the latest one from England

and you tell me that you're scared
your body won't hold up
hauling ass with hoses all over the city
the tough route, truck loads, 2am start
how you feel cornered, pressured about not moving out
your housemate needs you, is falling apart
needs the rent money to avoid eviction
that you think she's addicted to anxiety meds
getting sicker without the health care

and you talk about the pressures of our 86 year old dad
his nightly calls, Friday movie dates
last minute requests to come fix the computer, a fuse, haul groceries
his plan for the two of you to live together in some condo
how you can't seem to puncture his improbable
even though it will kill

and how at night you don't sleep because of the cough
but the doctor at the managed care place hasn't listened

and I tell you we need to go back
insist on a new diagnosis
book into a treatment program
even though they keep resisting, say *we are too full
have wait lists*
but you remind me of the three past attempts paid
out of your own money and our dad's
how you failed them
or they failed you

and yes, I remember the $15,000 plus a shot places
that demoralized me when I came for the family sessions
their business industry model
the one that let you take up with a woman there
who had a history of alcoholism right under their noses
another that expelled you for talking back to a worker
the perfunctory family sessions I drove hours to attend

and I get upset listening to you recount about your boss
the way he screams, fires people
then turns a blind eye, tans for months in the tropics
the misdiagnosis by your doctor
while your night couch persists
and wonder as I take in your longing, your pain
whether our compassion dozes
where we have come to America
where we are heading.

You wear cologne

but don't dance with anyone
won't set foot in a restaurant, a gym
blow a paper horn at a holiday party

wear your cologne
as if some ubiquitous good time waits
as if a girl will slide out of a donut shop
who needs a decent man
or the monkey lady dealer who needs
many men and for a bundle of money
spoils them to death.

You dab on cologne
after your fifty plus hour work week
after the pepperoni pizza, ballpark franks
your political wise cracks
your wicked witch of the west impersonation
after the green face bloated from gobbling children
rotates her head mechanically
in the corner of your room.

You wear cologne
it is shower fresh
rebukes a hard day
the bruised child
in a big person's body,
smacks of balsam
balmy weather
a cabin in the woods.

You can recite the Bill of Rights
cock a revolver
break a bread board in two
soothe ordinary folks
be the generous uncle
will never grow old

will absence the cologne that morning 9am, January 21
when the crematorium operator tells my father he can
pull the switch
but he doesn't pull the switch on your body
in its casket with the spill of red and yellow roses
that's been slid into the big steel oven
and will be burnt to a crisp
in three days come back
a plastic baggy of ashes.

You used to dab your neck with cologne.
It smelt of alpine air, the north country.
I'd stall my body in it
watch you walk unassuming
with your limp
ordinary jeans

your blue Jesus eyes
that nested the birds.

Your all-wheel drive

is New England Patriot protected
busts over rutted roads
is immoderate with gas
but who's saying.
Nobody is about to mess with it.
The car smells of Calvin Klein *Be* cologne
the stuff you buy by the box load
a mantra you propagate
on contrite knees

scent yourself shower fresh
amid the blue scaffolds
slow cruise up 82nd Avenue where
the cheap motels offer up 50 buck rooms
dollar tacos
drug dealers, pawn shops
and once in a while a dishy blonde
who doesn't object to your meatball subs, pizza.

You are a panther in your disguise hoodie
neat beard
six pack of Pepsi tucked inside the cooler
will swear by God
you are on your third life

that maybe it's not virtue that saves
or a borrowed 45 magnum
or the way the motel manager dishes drugs
tonight I have something special for you

or how your dungarees fit
or the over virtuous exercise routines of the righteous
or the neon electrified roller coaster

but maybe the way you escape things
will cut off an arm
amputate a leg
drag a knee held together with steel pins
Houdini the past
fly off wood ramps, town piers
with your jacked up wheels
aerial handshakes

fly like a banshee after igniting dynamite
rise up past hard surfaces
a cramped life

escape death again and again and again
by sheer determination
some immaculate white powdered stranger

that hounds the home of your mouth.

It's hard to be sleepless

not use palliatives
curse the wind for looting
for leaving you to rot on 82nd Avenue
with the pushers and prostitutes
the cops who come late
turn an invisible eye on the bruising.

But you will never come back
worship the god of hope
that shimmies out of a chemical turnstile
will never again feed dealers
gold watches, credit cards
car titles they don't deserve.

See how you flee
one stroke at a time
the way the medical doctors say
just acid reflex, up the pills
see how they race after you
as if pots of gold are a beehive

as if in our mercenary we are nothing
but a cold wind
white powder in a wine glass.

You have found a circuitous way to paradise

clutch it to your lips
let it travel your skin
obsequious

patron saint the hard measure
of your work days
the truck driving, oil fumes
endless loss
till they never talk nasty

travel you to a place where euphoria reigns
no woman is an iodine field
just fertile summer
and in her arms you are sinking.

You are my mother's soft fold
derailed child
daredevil on a motor bike
the kid who ruffles fate
taunts heaven with a matchstick.

I am your one sister, only sibling
never will get to say goodbye
your pale blue heart
my pale blue heart

the so much history we share

the way you climb soap boxes
catch the wind

dig out a father's reprisals
the day's unseemly

move fast as lightning
attempt to leave him in a thin dust
with the velocity of your wings.

The night you try to commit suicide

on crack in the motel room
call to say *goodbye*
is the night I will cry and beg
behind the jazz club

beg for an address
plead for an address
say *don't leave me*
I need to see you
is the night you say
Be happy, I'm going back to her

and I will beg and cry more
till finally you give the name of the motel
and we drive across town to 82nd
and my father is only later allowed up
and then you will say what you've never said–
Hey, still act like a big man now...
did it feel good hitting me
making me fist fight other boys in our yard....
and he will reply with his resolute lips –
somebody had to knock some sense into you

is the same night you will lunge for him
your anger almost uncontainable
but not hit
and my friend visiting from England
who has prayed with you

will calm you down,
the brother god watches over
who's on his seventh life
does not get taken down
by the massive crack dose

is the same night you will soothe my dad
let him drive
stay overnight on the couch
say you didn't mean it
sorry, I shot off my mouth
next morning make him
hash browns, sausage

and none of us will know
that six months from now
after using and using and using
hauling our 86 year old father to
movies, groceries, meals
listening nightly to his phone calls
fixing his DVD player, bathroom sink, clocks
you will drop dead
of supposed heart failure
in another anonymous motel room.

Part Three

Patronage

Sometimes we write others off

decide they'll never grow a fertile field
avoid black spot, locust
their lack of guile isn't enough.
They are castoff trees in a sea of shine
live on the leftovers of our gleaming.

My brother walks with a limp.
works a hard shitty job
won't make it to his 50th birthday
is a casualty of punch cards
our penchant for self-made
bare bones healthcare
a school that never noticed him
a train yard of jobs
everybody saying *what a hard worker*
while he limps out of buildings
is too shy to eat in a restaurant
join a gym
goes home to his invisible.

My brother is a landscape
of cattle cars and clear cuts
what gets lost.

How many expensive drug treatment programs
with no subsidies
how many anonymous hospital rooms with
the pain of his back crippling
his pleas, my pleas and pleas and pleas

yet to be turned away
how many days and nights gone missing?

So many funny pop-up cards and crisp $100 bills
for his one niece and nephew
the fixed car radiators, last minute babysitting.
How does a good heart end
up in a twister

where can anyone of us go when
the night slurs, speaks dirty?

You will barely eat the Christmas meal

I already know that
the fasting and denial
the way you fret your body won't
fit into the eye of a needle.

Afterwards I offer up dessert –
fruitcake, apple pie and ice cream
oranges
but you are not taking

have always denied the daily bread
then ravaged your body on hot dogs, pizza
when the night gets murky.

You will barely eat this holiday
never go on vacation
walk a beach
lay out in the yard
just work like a pack mule
beg overtime
take on everything they can strap

wake up midnight, drive forty minutes
to get to your locker, overalls
the hoses, truck
bring no lunch bucket
only a blue cooler loaded with soda.

You are fasting again.
It is Christmas.
Your plate looks big
the helpings do not.

I can count the years I have watched you
haul ass with a disguised limp
travel a stiff spine after the back surgery
the way you never want your almost fifty to show
will take on any job, any weight
become the workhorse employee
can crush an oil can with your fist
riot the office

suck up restaurant grease
that will become biodiesel
crash on the sofa by seven
then up again late night to run the hoses
all over the city in your big truck

as if working to death
doesn't mean anything
is part of this trip
won't mangle.

You hold an invisible guardrail

look for steady
permanency that defies the
vanishing of the breadsticks.

If I could negotiate hell
treatise the territory of drug dealers
would I be able to save
open you onto a green field
scarlet your priestly
disrobe the woman in the glass bed

would the ring fit
the peonies come to meet you
the sun be more than a stab of death
open onto whippoorwills
the night sky spun into Van Gogh's
swirl of indigo

if I could pole-vault over
the raised and raped earth
its stump fields, famine's dim robes
stroke the boy inside the man's weeping
cover you in mother of snow

would you pull away
or do what any ordinary child
on a mother's lap is prone to
pool in the good milk
purse your lips
over her pearled white elocution
and drink?

Sometimes you and I don't seem alike

travel different geography
your polar ice caps, my books of poems

your work boots, my sculptures of women
your greasy pizza next to my bagged veggies.

Sometimes a kid brother can oust the moon
street talk the dark
find nobody listens
forget child kingdoms.
Sometimes all the chocolate coins in the world
won't end up a success story.

I gather cilantro, fan your absence
like you, want the holy grail
but our paths grew different.

You and I know how the dark feels
when the world is not pretty
when decency is a hijacked bride
ragged coat

know there are seven swear words
for every frill one
that the earth lost three beats
when the sun went vacant.

I know you are riding a fragile pony
across the western frontier

its dry dust and watering holes
I know I know   I know
but I am sick for your safety
want no more moon missing.

The day journey is hard

heavy shoes, a 2am start
grease cans and sooted overalls
truck stop after truck stop
twenty five of them all over the city
before today's route is done.

Is it surprising our lives
grow weary
get lost in coffee, big fries
pill box houses
a polite yard

that you won't last
will die young like my mother
peeled from the heart's green field
that my father will plant dirt
in your work boots
worship their soiled buff
chewed soles
that out of the creased hills
will come stabs of crocus

that he will hero worship your life
as if it were a bullet on a train
recount your diligence
Friday afternoon movie dates
how for years your back hurt

your leg dragged
but you didn't succumb
didn't succumb

managed to surmount
the torn angle
of your body's enclaves.

Your body is tired

from being bulldozed
expected to lift weight, lug hoses
truck drive the miles.

You are a disguised field of marigold
the rain trespassed
blue eyed boy in need of a mission.

In the heroic world are we more than
screen tinsel, palpitated longing
does Spiderman wax perfect
do you surmount floods, scale buildings
call to task the maul of thugs
that threaten to overtake Crimson City?

Some people are poised for action
before the world is ready
are their mother's child
deserted when she vanishes
with her blue crystal.

See how infamous we can feel
pistol perfect
married to a wallet of bills

mount each day
grow indomitable
cancel the past, our defeats
become such steel throated nightingales.

You garble your words

they are
the detritus time leaves
after it rapes us

they are
the abandoned schoolyard
broken mother
pistoled fantasies
of a blue halo.

See how exodus feels
not exile
the measureless of the world
beyond this glass

the way the stars weep
carry you home
without asking.

They want your name

spelled properly
someone to identify the body
lay you to rest in your red check shirt
ordinary jeans

hand me a zip locked bag
that holds life's scant excesses –
$28 in bills and change
your thin leather wallet
a set of keys

show me a picture
of your body spread out on the motel bed
the nearly full glass of pepsi
your shirt off
the sheets neat as a pin
the bedspread turned down careful
your silver wire glasses paused on your forehead
as if you went off to sleep in a gentle haze.

Everybody wants me to believe this
that you went quietly of your own volition
heart failure, unnoticed in a motel room
no foul play
no reason your gold watch, expensive hoodie are missing
and the unfamiliar woman you arrived with is missing
that the guys shouting obscenities, railing at your
front door
in the middle of the night

with their threats of revenge
have nothing to do with this

that probably nothing will ever get suspected
be spoken of
my father, going on 86, will recount your career
as a hard worker, decent son who will deny
a lifetime of hurt
find a condo with him come April
place with a patch of sun, patio, cable television.
And I will never tell this old man the truth about
what my brother has told me
will not go into the fears, anguish my brother's been living
the 45 he'd borrowed and kept by his side
on guard sitting in the living room sleepless
the fact he told me *my life is in jeopardy*

that guys like this who deal white powder tricks
are not afraid to break a nose, poison a coke.

The medical examiner guesses you went quietly
congestive heart failure
shows me your morgue picture
the dry white crusted around your lips
suggests we do no autopsy
close the book, arrange the funeral
keep my father's memories intact

leave undisturbed
whatever we know and don't know
about the night of your death.

Part Four

Pallbearer

The crops went fallow

the day you died
birds bent the sky
geese knelt
yard hoses emptied.

Sure, I had rehearsed death
its blue tallow, maudlin teeth
but this was the real thing
your 6'3" body in the morgue
a zip lock bag handed to me
$28 in bills, a few coins
cell phone, couple of keys.

There is no way to prepare.
Your car sits
in a motel parking lot
needs to be moved
there are funeral arrangements
your job to call
relatives, friends.

My father's face is shattered.
I sit in the car speechless
as if no available light saves
as if I am *not* angry
at the years of holes you have dug
the luckless life
cold chill of America.

You will never grow old

never stop being the guy with the hoses
who sucks up polluted restaurant oil
drives all over the city in a big truck

will never grow tired of pizza, election jokes
talking the piss with the penitentiary guards
tire of the way the women in the yard
eye you in your blue coveralls.

You will never again deal with the angry neighbor
have to move your car because it's parked
two inches over the allotted space

will never tire of paying the rent
the no life insurance
working to support the owner's Palm Beach lifestyle

will never hunger and thirst after money
buy a new car
imagine some big time vacation in Maui
grow thin on your poor man's salary

will never again need to use deodorant
launder the thick grease off your work clothes
listen to your housemate stress over the cost of meds.

The fog, car pollution, weather, cough won't tire
you'll get to breath easy

there won't be any hope for cashmere
the chance for kids
no swollen demand for diapers, air guns
swing sets, a woman's negligee

you won't have to mend the yard hose
my car radiator
go out in the Northwest rain to get mail

your clothes will now and forever
fit the same
the dinner you ate yesterday will turn out
to be enough
the dog will still wait by the door

I will call to you
call to you
call to you

and like an evening rain
that taps taps as it falls
wish you were still coming back.

They are trying to keep your flesh pink

not tawdry
no embalming
so the art of makeup becomes a nuanced affair.
At the funeral my kids do not want to see.
I step in the wake room and bury a note
an alabaster heart in the satin folds of your casket.

You wear a simple white tee, polo
worn in jeans
no shoes or socks
do not look in pain, overworked
perfunctory.

A few days from now we will watch
the casket move on a rail of wheels
the blue inferno.
My father needs to see this
before he can sleep
know for sure it's not an anonymous oven
generic ashes.

I will go home and eat popcorn.
Have dreaded this day for years
kept myself arm's length
used to say *Chris, don't leave me! Stay!*
but my voice grew weary.

You always had a mind of your own.
Kept going   going   going
till you were gone.

You want me to be a pallbearer

before my time
bury my love
that has survived hailstorms
circumnavigates your trees.

If epoxy could keep us together
then we would be sad twins
who understand loss
palpitate disaster

but our paths diverted

when you navigated the trenches
and I grew thirsty for another kind of scenery.

The whistle blower has never been able
to get enough of you.

I comb the field

remember your Ray-Ban shades
sketchbook, scout pins
pockmarked tees
dungarees folded neat in the drawer
how you cut and pasted
cut and pasted
searched for a good fit

and I am amazed how spare a life can be
its plastic hangers, no camera, stereo
cheap cell phone, potato chips
its polar ice caps, fair-thee-wells
grease traps
tongue and grooved
how easy it settles into a couple of boxes

and I am sad how quickly what we love
waves goodbye
becomes the doctor's misdiagnosis
melted ice in a cocktail
the colicky child
molested stranger
bue ray fantasy on a blank screen.

I do not want to suds the past

stab lust to a metal cupid
kitchen kettle love
till it whistles on cue
above the stove flame

do not want to cargo trunk rooms
blindfold the sky
as if god is missing

do not say *yes* to your death –
not even close
busy bee the day
somebody came
stabbed your heart
knotted a voicemail

day the sun wept
and the rain shriveled

do not say *life goes on*
I'm about to buy a new dog
marvel at the blood red allegiance of roses
the way your casket slides into the oven
flames the dark

refuses to keep up
with our no nonsense
pitch perfect.

Your body will be burned

in the corrugated gray box
with a famine of yellow roses
ash to ash
within three hours there will be
nothing much left.
They ask my 86 year old dad if he wants
to press the metal switch.
He has insisted on being here
at the anonymous office building
that hides a crematorium, big ovens
a panel of knobs
but when given the choice to be executioner
shakes his head solemnly, says *no*.

How many roads are there to death?
Is there the slow and the fast lane
the puff sports car that veers off the side rail
the empty bread bowl
the crumbled cane of a man
who lives with the memory of two dead wives
rocks to shift his weight out of the chair?

Are there the in-between deaths
that are half detritus, half pomegranate
and the small deaths that come pall mall
through a lifetime, nearly seize us
the car that almost jumped the curb
the cancer that creeps up uninvited
the hand grenades and slow weeping

the rabid dog
the close call with pneumonia
the ski fall that managed to lean just
the right side of paralysis

are there the invisible deaths too
that nearly claim us
the shrunken marriage
child lost to a grownup's street mall
the monotonous of the technology
the way her face looked thirty years ago
before the early heart attack
the vaporous job
the infidelities that wore the wolverine of winter
but secretly courted April

and are there deaths by attrition
the dice cast too late
the road we refused with its margin
of wild roses
the forever waiting
the hand unoffered
the fossilized child
the way indecision feels when
the glove doesn't fit and we are caught
in somebody else's windfall?

How many roads to death are there
how many chicken salad sandwiches
Elvis Presley songs
yoyos and glue guns

peridots the color of summer
how many lost voices, forgotten voices
did you hear that exclamation marks
scribbled notes
trapped shoes
first kisses that never
foretell the last

how many fled Gabriels
hands that marry the dark
dime store rings and water pistols
how many rock collections
rubber bugs
travelogues of Greta singing

how many roads to home
roads to call *home*.

You were buried

on a day filled with bright sun
the 18${}^{\text{th}}$ of January.
Some days stick with me like fly paper
always look back.

I have spent my life in a cold landscape
lived far from pried open sky
imagine my hands staked to your field
the marionberries, Swiss chard
summer squash ripening
your voice invader of a light filled room
endless lovemaking.

When I worship you
you are the god of light and pomegranates
aren't fussy about your clothes
go on long walks amid the velvet.
There is no hard bed
nails in your hands
no cross bearing you home
in the rain of this tired century.

The breakfast of the dead

is taken without vows
crows swoop down
peck dirt
the once cereal version of paradise
sits defunct at the curb.

I hound your epistolary
offer up incense
lathe your body in oil
honeysuckle
watch the coffin turn to ash
at the flick of a switch.

Once you could see in the dark
flashed bright as a glow worm
fluorescent
my mother's lips coated you
there was no cadence of brokenness.

Once you built wood ramps
climbed a fire escape
scraped rust off the sky
broke an arm reaching
almost impervious
inside her blue halo.

Part Five

A Praxis of Want

We have bought cast hearts

heavy as rock.
They sit on brass stands
have screws in the back
will swing open to lick up your ashes
bought one cloisonné urn
small as a child toy
for my twenty year old son
who loved you special.

We have bought shaved hope
that runs barefoot
complains of the rain

have bought guerilla pants
and sugar pantomimes
cowboy boots that squish
the dark without swearing

have sewn your body into
a permanent bathrobe
that never rusts

no more hunched over
a heavy workload
grease monkey's epitaph

see how your cleaned up
ruddy face shines
the way we dig dirt out of your nails

lay your big hands to rest
and your beautiful blue eyes

see how we decommission the wasp nests
shiny trumpet dealers
lay you to sleep
ever so tender.

Your voice

will never grow impatient
want off the phone
get tired of hearing about my lovesick
your seat at the family Easter meal.

Your voice has gone quiet.
No more impersonations
stories about the down on their luck
immigrant families, axed jobs,
the prison yard
rats some kitchens must conceal

no more predictions about El Nino
continental plate shifts, American supremacy
the thinned ice cap.

You have always cataloged catastrophes
daredevil heroics, car stunts
men in underwater cages who
uncuff from a ball and chain
swim to the surface, gulp air
as if at the last moment
god decides to be good to them.

Your voice will never again populate Christmas
call for Chinese takeout
tease your nephew into giggles
deny the big helpings of mashed potato
chicken, bread rolls
hours later eat Sicilian pizza
hot dogs doused with liquid cheese, ketchup.

You understood wounded birds, hurt children
time bombs.
I have always wanted to protect you
see you lift above the stone wall
find your aerial
have always wanted to erase the back break jobs
medical bills, endless slog
the nothing to show for it
nothing to show for it
just a couple of cardboard boxes
movable keepsakes

have wanted to see you make honey
from your beehive
lounge in a slope chair
with a view of the trees.

For years now, since our mother died
I've wanted to protect you
haven't always known how.

February marches into April

with its blue mitt
sleeps with porcupine
the field's brittle
buries my dead brother
sinks his blue eyes
swallows him whole
as if the night is hungry.

See how toothy death can be
how it kneels to meet us
our chaparrals and carnivorous
refuses to take *No*
live life on a mock handshake.

See how death paralyzes the grass
annuls kittens
takes us through bandit country
lost in the stampede
lost in the stampede ....

till it claims.

It won't do any good

to soothe me
tell me *it's alright alright*
as if life is an air gun
goes where you aim
so our aim must be flawless.

It's no good telling me *you'll get over it*
as if a desiccated field can roll over
be seeded in Timothy
acid rain won't leak.

It's no good telling me *he brought it on himself*
because the story is bigger
and I will want to spit in your eye
for trivializing.

It's no good seeing someone die
when better luck
kinder employers
medical care
a compassionate America
might save.

See how the world looks from here –
so fleeting – dark
our lives not so invincible
the steady work of our lungs
our heart beat
no guarantee.

I'm kissing your hallelujah chorus

torn epitaphs, hand-me-downs
peridots that defy the
blue swales of winter.

There are electrified swans
but nobody is saying
a child left out in the cold
powdered white cake, a drug dealer's militia
but you are not saying

and as for the night
what if it swears by paralysis
and you scatter into a blue ocean
and her body is a field's length away
and she calls you
out of your shrapneled past
wants nothing to go missing

what if you can undo the past
wake up tomorrow comforted by flame
eggs and bacon
a country gone past empty pledges
if the poor man can speak for us
and she *is* still alive
barefoot in her blue kimono

what if the dark comes to you
out of an iced sky, weeps
rocks you in bed

what will death say then
as she sidles you
kisses you for her own
promises to never leave
never leave.

You are *not* knee deep in hand grenades

no one has yet signed off your death certificate
given away the new car
no child is at home waiting
no job will be unable to live without you
the day will go on
the losses will go on
what is consumed here
what multiplies

my life will stumble then go on
the clock will refuse to play truant
your housemate will weep, get someone for the room
the sun will come out
the rain drizzle
your niece and nephew will still travel street malls
pump out text messages
our dad will read the obituaries
work his crossword
stay up late night, obsess over why his only son
died alone in a motel room

I will still worship my mother's voice
its dissolved fluency
the way she swoops up hailstorms
vagrants our yard
refuses to take *no*
reigns and reigns like blue velvet
over the busted fuse of your heart.

It is your birthday

just a week since the funeral
and nothing seems right.
Sure, the day goes on, I buy bread
get my daughter the corsage for her dance
whisk eggs for an omelet
work my job, drive the endless
sure, you would want us to not fall prey
stay nimble
keep up
let the sun soothe.

It is your birthday.
You are now ageless
fired to ash in a wide oven
with the yellow and red roses
your workmen's hands, grey coffin
my alabaster heart.

Yesterday the funeral home called
said *we have Chris*
and for a moment I thought
you were alive
would walk out their door barefoot
hug me in your blue jeans, white tee

but it is the remains they hand me.
Ash unto ash
your body squashed into a plastic bag
green sack
and I don't want to feel the weight
believe this gravel and bone is the once you

as if we can bag a life
into plastic, a twist tie
obituary notice
combed words.

Today is your birthday.
Unlike me, you will never grow old
will be frozen in time

forever be my mother's only son
the child who baits bees
aerial jumps disaster
refuses to take No
baits death
works double time
chows down hot dogs, pizza
cracks jokes
underplays your smarts

ingests piles of white sugar
confuses what you need.

Your ashes are sealed

in a heart wreathed with ivy
can no longer perish.
It sits on a brass stand
but still I imagine you
calling home the birds.
And I know you are more than the ashes
more than a putrefied porcelain heart
brass bands, pull toys.

I place you in my forever
that is bigger than a brass stand
won't tarnish, need to arm wrestle the dark
ask you to deal cards, crack jokes
order your brand of pizza

place you away from the identical
jeans and jerseys, take-outs
grid streets lined with strip joints
anonymous neglect that renders you invisible.

See how I carry you across the mud spackled field
into first crocus
call your name as if the afternoon needs you
the day's petaled wings are your
carpetbagger's epiphany.

See how I call you call you call you
as if you are right here
only momentarily lost
in your boy sleep
about to wake
light up the sky
with your firecrackers.

This day holds the memory

of cornflakes
Nebraska sunsets
grain fields and the farmer's diligence

has your dime store pinwheels
that spin a shiny blade
factory flawless
motor bikes that flatten the wheat as you soar

holds the memory of a workman's hands
buff clothes, car wax
Buddha statutes, tribal drums left in
evacuated apartments.

My car has your axle grease
polarized sunglasses, skull lighter
the dangle of that paper tree
that spreads blue balsam
your plastic hula dancer
map of the coast.

The road has your razored hope
lost years, abutted years
stapled years
years of horseplay and speed tickets
paper box factories, rock quarries
pack horse hauling
always hauling
and hands at the end of the day

so embedded with dirt
you let the chemicals peel them.

My words have your antidotes in them
your ochre sunsets, pall mall excuses
poorboy sandwiches
the way you court death
one tease
slip of paper at a time
tinsel taunt
white powdered homilies.

Your life has that *don't get too attached*
quality
reminds me -
things come and go
slip from our permanence.

Your voice has that soothing
see in the dark quality
the incredulous married to
the matter-of-fact
your red fuse
courtship with dynamite
riffs on a blue guitar
your riotous, rubbed clean
corpulent and gone.

If the sun blessed your face

would I forget the grey maul of winter
its horsehair, banished Lucretius
briar of slumped down roses
the epistolary of want that tears open
every combed room
would the crisis of the birds go
unheeded by me?

I eat salt, want to become ocean
watch the seasons run together
like paste beads
till all puddles are the kingdom
of backyard boats
cropped skirts and life jackets
the silver glean of the children shouting
The sea! The sea!

In the Northwest
January wears webbed feet
the sky cripples.
The woman up the path yells *stop*
to her six year old
pizza slices slide out of glass doors
endless coffee
sex turns difficult in the ice bed
we want to believe everyone needs us
that, like the sun, we are the glean
that brightens somebody else's winter

that today nothing will fail
the early crocus will climb ringless
avoid calamity

no one will shotgun the crows
the neighbor watering broccoli sprouts
will stave off the cancer
strangers arrive
derelict cars turn gemstone
the mistreated child angles a new home

want to believe life goes on
not maverick as runaway shoes
but nascent to nightfall
to your daughter's egg salad sandwiches
the dog's habitual
this séance of winter
its glum face, rock salt.

Then, when you arrive at my door vagrant
unabashed glitter queen in a blue haze
I will stop everything
drop to the pavement as if worship
is a three letter word, I am your servant
and maybe my brother's death, the funeral
will seem like a thousand miles away.

I will sit on the concrete
spell my body in psalm
watch my mother's face open
let words flee
take you and take you
till nobody is home
and the birds arrive
nest easy in my dead brother's hair.

Some of us walk the world

in search of sweetmeat
live on a tightrope
meet a valley of lead.

In October our kitten went missing.
No trace.
My son put it down to possum.
The German cuckoo clock my father gave me
with its revolving children, waterwheel
was finally screwed up on the wall
but the gears stopped and now the bird
refuses to come out of her carved window.
My brother will absentee Thanksgiving
limp his way into Christmas
says he can't sleep nights because of the cough.

Almost everyone in my family has died young
but I'm not counting.
Sometimes it takes more than a livable wage
new car, job title, grade inflation
smooth your butt/tone your abs gym workout
more than a faithless husband who entertains
late night brunettes, porn
Pulitzer Prize winning love emails.

The radio spiel gets on my nerves
as if nobody hurts
needs to slut

bury the past in crack cocaine
sell their watches, stereo
suck kitchen oil into big hoses
dig rock out of the earth

as if want doesn't maim things
and some dumbed down redundant
electronic version of a melody
is the only one that will stick
pump our life into a sport bed
multimillion dollar celebrity.

Sometimes the words around me
neuter, embalm children
get pasted on a metal shank
industrial.

Sometimes your voice struts
hips flash, my under slip goes missing.
I parade in a forest
dream the Blue Danube
Sappho before the rain
dream nothing is futile, gone in smoke
about to be missing,
my brother buys a cabin
snowshoes over his past, virgin snow
meets a good woman
ceremonies the cold.

I stop believing the world is sepia
gets yanked on a harsh chain.

Sometimes the dark seems bearable
the room gets spot cleaned miraculous
death loses its grip
sinks into the sky, sings.
I don't fight the fact my brother
will go missing
disappear in a puff
two weeks after Christmas
on the anniversary of my mother's death

instead watch him skate the pond
gather a fistful of new snow
from the cup of his hands
lick white crystal.

The auburn in your hair

that rests beside the grey
will never turn color
not like the cardboard box that holds
a life's keepsakes
toy sized convertible, plastic dinosaur
two DVD's, book of my poems
oval frame with our mom dressed in her pillbox hat,
fake fur
a few funny greeting cards, motorcycle magazines
copies of your resume that show you are a hard worker
can drive truck, fork lift, haul gravel
do apartment maintenance
fix heat, cooling, electric systems, cars.

The auburn in your hair beside the grey
will never turn color
and as for your eyes, those soft blue eyes
they are reduced to memory's rubble
to the incinerator's impartial
reduced to a heavy plastic bag I have buried
because I can't face dealing with that trip to the coast
where your ashes will join my mother's ashes
finger for her in the foam of the waves.

The auburn in your hair
once foretold Indian paintbrush
the October dazzle of red and gold
New England foliage

once foretold good omens
a god given to prayer wheels
the blue warbler
brazen jay at the yard feeder
was the cackle of cock and crow
the soft nuzzle of my mother
the unending calm of the field.

PART SIX

The Diurnal Sunset

The diurnal sunset

you once imagined
will never come true
nor any more fire in your limbs
log cabins
a woman who gifts you
with suppers of pork chop
kids' play.

The spirit of you will always be two parts pizza
a snowy trek through the woods.
But now you sleep easy.
The black flies don't bite.
You don't need to shave, count calories
disguise your limp.
French fries will never again tempt.
The monkey lady that burns hearts is
relegated to a side yard.
The climate of love no longer rolls dice.

The diurnal sunset you once imagined
will still spread across the Wisconsin skyline
annul chores
stun children
make the couple on the hill fondle
pause the peck of their kisses
help the dying man forget cancer
cancel momentarily the bills
divorce papers, house payments
the way death derails
will fan us with its splintered glory
purple, coral, blue, ochre
before the dark.

Some people burn so bright

the flames eat them
they are scarlet wealth on a stippled day
a brazen trumpet,
they are not my brother
who in his tee shirt, ordinary jeans
manages to slide in and out of doors
with nobody noticing.

I've been sounding a blue note
to call him home
but he doesn't hear

as if elocution fails me
his broken bones
emptied birthdate.

And the primroses
what have become of them
orphaned waifs
do they populate his garden
call him back
drink nectar from a paper straw?

Your hair is windswept

from traveling.
I ask what it is like.
You don't seem dismal
defeated as caged animals
bereft with loss
hungry for a day's meal.
The blood clots in your leg
the metal pins aren't hurting.

You are windswept
from traveling
have been a lot of miles
in a few days
dropped in on my mother
talked the peonies out of hiding
walked the beach

as if you and I aren't swimless
are blue fins
green plankton
the rhythm of waves.

You are windswept
from traveling.
I am not sure
where you are heading
what port waits,
pause in the ripple
of your wake.

You are a pebble field

waxwing the world with silence
now that your spare words
have slipped into the woods
and the river of death litters.

Your face has grown fluid
spills blue light over the parking lot
over the woman bagging groceries
the boy accused of shoplifting
the old man's stiff leg
soothes the sodden
is not sanctimonious

sets up no bandstands
waxed treatises
no barbed wire, bomb squads

like the pebble field
on the warmed afternoon of a January day
your heart has spilt open
hums.

Your death is a broad machine

over an orphaned plain
sharp glass
luck's lost stethoscope.

I call your name
as if the dark retrieves things
unburies a ruddy face
bike ramp
her blue cradle

as if every room is more than
a serialized version of loss
lifetime of useless name stickers.

Your death holds buckled rails
the tease of first crocus
lamb stew my father makes
to still the pain of his weeping

holds the fastness of cars racing
that one faithful nightingale in the tree.

Do you still peel the top off

your blue convertible
give race lessons
spit polish chrome

hustle frisbees, burger joints
pool tables
flirt with girls from Malaysia

ride the roadway past topless bars
horse farms, wine country?

Now that the yellow roses
spewed across your grey casket
have grown back

do you lounge beside tray tables
water the hyacinth

watch the cousin dolls bob
then smooch on the car console
fix the neighbor's radiator

remind me to flirt the moon
travel a Shropshire sunset
not miniature lovemaking

will I still see you there
the plaid shirted journeyman
my baby brother
that spark of mischief

racing like a banshee
through the honey ripe
tall as your thigh
field?

Some days do you aerate the yard

poke holes
haul paper, twigs
twine a house with loose windows
hypnotize summer into staying
propagate a past that speaks kind?

Some things are a refutation of
combed elocution
divorce rings
a fenced landscape.

Some days have no rest to them.
No vanilla, spotted dog, pantomime.

I save last year's lavender in a glass case
the memory of your hands in snow
the fields of lupine you planted
in my children's day book.

When I braille you in the dark

you offer up snow
blue cotlettes
no field of ash.
We pace round each other.
I curse your absence
sloped body
veiled trees

tell you the pro sunglasses
have gone to pay bills
that it's hard to speak your name
my children miss you
will grow up without an uncle
hold onto a few mementos
a brass frame with your pic
box cars, sports insignia
want to remember your decent heart
generous love
wounded by shrapnel

and I tell you
you can't go up in smoke
need to keep trucking
hang around my inveterate
scoop up flies
resettle them outdoors
remind me of the value of wind farms

that like you, I am a small peg in a square hole
don't always understand the world
could go up in smoke
but my soul's not willing

that there are so many miles
to steer a good life

but sometimes we get marooned
the hieroglyphs of the moon fail.

Chris – can you see the rain on the roof splatter
first of the red tail come back to pilfer
the holly's holy devotion to dirt
the crypt of my heart
place you have picked clean
with the sovereignty of your white fingers?

We pace round each other
you and I
are *not* the blind leading the blind
the torn mantras of love
in a wax work place
we are memory's favorite cousin
as we run and rip with the breeze
collect fire flies
shape our Queens summers
into the water hydrant of playground
bike and bike and bike
till even the dark needs us
does not curse.

The ghosts of the dark

are not fussy
chalk the wall
ingest night poems
the street man's vigil
canned ham, kerosene

catalog the cat's one eye
the couple that worships lust
then maims it.

The ghosts of the dark
toss down queens
hound aces, a straight run
pool chips on a blue salver.

Every day I look death in the face
gather its leaf fall
runt pups
the way loss gropes
ices her body till it freezes

thank any stranger for asking.

The dark can be blinding

but so is love
the messy of it
the way citrus stings
and death plagues
unremitting as bird call.

I can see in the night
preternatural
the blind leading the blind
can see your dozed face
how it looks in the cheap casket
with the buffer of yellow roses

can see the brine and calm of you
my father's pressed lips

the way the cold no longer harms

your talced hands
folded benevolence

how in the shadow
one pale angel sings.

It is hard to make a life fit

into a boot box
canon the dark
cram scenery
the pock mocks, blue Jesus
keep from stapling want
to a thin sunset
rain drenched nights in Hoquim
drug treatment
the way homeless feels
down to the last $10 bill.

It's hard to cram a life into loose-leaf
handhold the beach at Rockaway
the bathing beauties of Galveston
paper parades
morels picked in the Coast Range
the size of Wisconsin pumpkins
a Flagstaff winter
do them all well.

It's hard to mine a life
dig out the dross
fool's gold, moratoriums
down and outs
faux fur married to fun fairs
the glass poodles
shake it up rattle and rare breeds.

Your memories can go on forever
truant the dark
suckle a day bed
rub clean the labored past
anoint a father
till he is no longer the abandoned child
busted fuse
grows almost hopeful
almost hopeful

is kissed by his son, my brother
blue haloed
till nothing looks cursed.

Who calls the dark out of hiding

arrests the snow

tools the sky's rose bushes

who pardons fate
as if the monograms of hope
never die?

Listen my friend –
the stars singe
the moon unbuttons her throat
for us.

It's time for you to start

playing the ukulele
no more pussy footing

I've imagined you learning
an instrument
want to see you strum
to your heart's content

serenade hyacinth
a good woman
the pocket moon
slant of window.

It's time for you to start
learning the ukulele

you play
   I will listen.

Toni Thomas lives in Portland, Oregon. Her poems have appeared in literary magazines in Austria, Spain, New Zealand, Canada, England, Scotland, and Australia. In the United States her work has been accepted for publication in over fifty literary magazines, including Prairie Schooner, North Dakota Quarterly, Hayden's Ferry Review, the Minnesota Review, Weber-The Contemporary West, Rhino, Notre Dame Review, and Poetry East.

She has published four other poetry collections – *Chosen, Fast as Lightning, Walking on Water* and *Ace Raider of the Unfathomable Universe*. Her work has received numerous awards and twice been nominated for a Pushcart Prize.

When she is not writing poems, Toni enjoys sculpting clay. Her figurative pieces have been shown in gallery and museum exhibits in Portland and Chicago, displayed in literary magazines, and housed in private collections in the U.S. and England.

Since Toni remains buried in poems and manuscripts, she likes to imagine all of them out in the world thick as wild lupin swaying.

She can be contacted at www.tonithomaspoetry.com

www.ingramcontent.com/pod-product-compliance
Lightning Source LLC
Chambersburg PA
CBHW052134010526
44113CB00036B/2222